D0945089

AFRICAN BUFFALO

Maddie Gibbs

Published in 2011 by The Rosen Publishing Group, Inc.
29 East 21st Street, New York, NY 10010

First Edition

Editor: Amelie von Zumbusch
Layout Design: Greg Tucker

Photo Credits: Cover Anup Shah/Digital Vision/Thinkstock; pp. 5, 11, 24 (bottom left) Hemera/Thinkstock; pp. 7, 13, 15, 17, 19, 21, 23, 24 (top left, top right) Shutterstock.com; pp. 9, 24 (bottom right) iStockphoto/Thinkstock.

Library of Congress Cataloging-in-Publication Data

Gibbs, Maddie.
 African buffalo / by Maddie Gibbs. — 1st ed.
     p. cm. — (Safari animals)
 Includes index.
 ISBN 978-1-4488-2508-0 (library binding) — ISBN 978-1-4488-2604-9 (pbk.) —
ISBN 978-1-4488-2605-6 (6-pack)
 1. African buffalo—Juvenile literature. I. Title.
 QL737.U53G524 2011
 599.64'2—dc22
                              2010023592

Manufactured in the United States of America

CPSIA Compliance Information: Batch #WW11PK: For Further Information contact Rosen Publishing, New York, New York at 1-800-237-9932

Contents

This is an African buffalo.
African buffalo are also
known as Cape buffalo.

5

As you might guess from their name, African buffalo live in Africa.

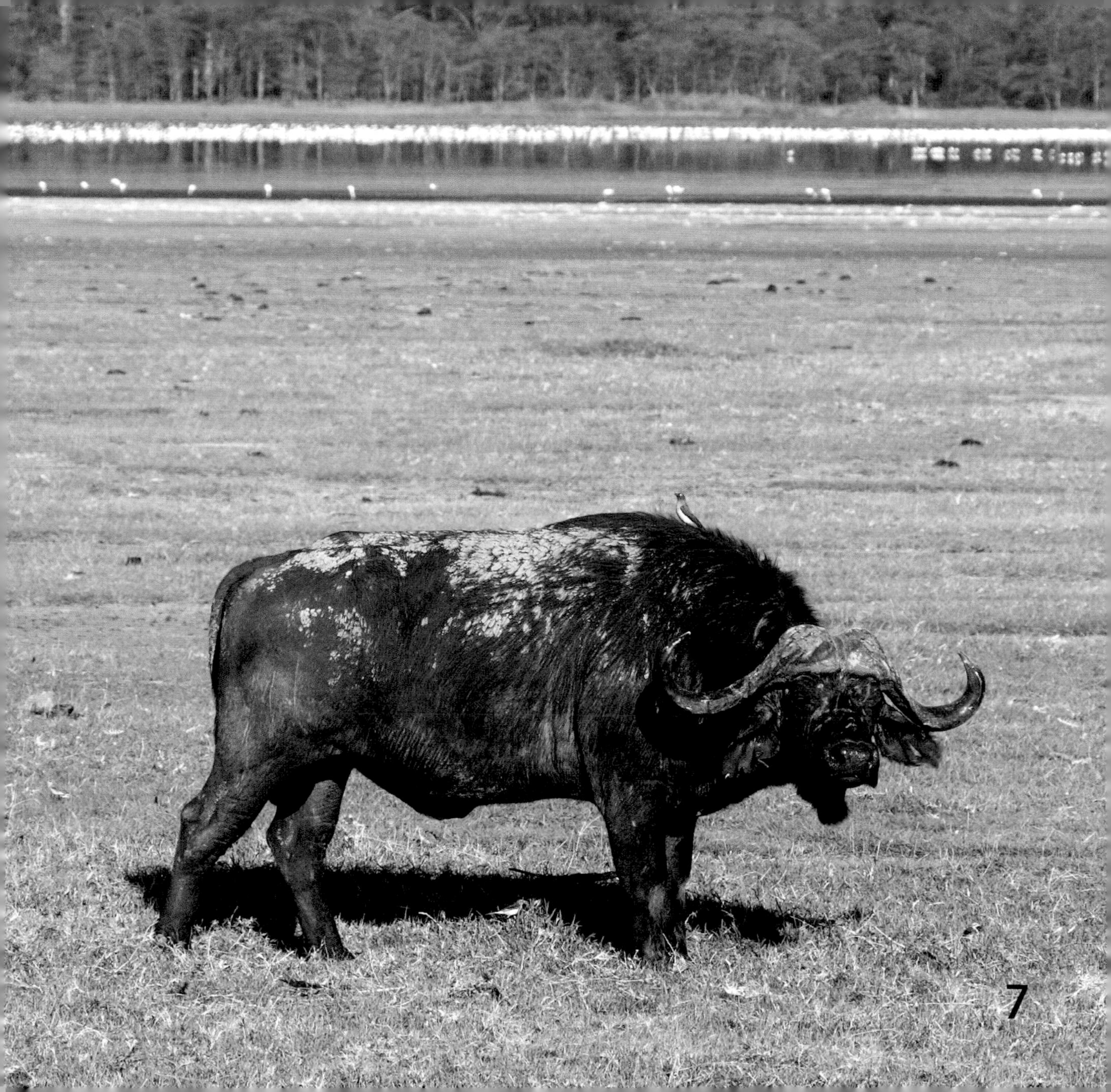

Some African buffalo live in forests. Others live on the open **savanna**.

9

Both male and female African buffalo have **horns**.

These buffalo are strong. They are a danger to animals that try to hunt them.

African buffalo eat plants, such as grass. Their stomachs have four sections.

17

African buffalo need to drink water every day. They also swim in water to cool off.

19

African buffalo form large **herds** with hundreds or thousands of members.

21

Young African buffalo are called **calves**. Calves drink their mothers' milk.

23

Words to Know

calf

herd

horn

savanna

Index

Web Sites

Due to the changing nature of Internet links, PowerKids Press has developed an online list of Web sites related to the subject of this book. This site is updated regularly. Please use this link to access the list: www.powerkidslinks.com/safari/afbuff/